GROWING UP ON A DEER FARM

By Karen Shellhaas

COPYRIGHT 2012

Printed in the United States of America - Charleston, SC

Library of Congress Catalog Card Number: 2012902902

ISBN-13: 978-1468112757

ISBN-10: 1468112759

For more information about the book, please visit website:

www.deerfawnbook.com

Hi, I'm Zack, a baby **white-tail** fawn. I am called a white-tail because the underside of my tail has pure white fur. That's my twin sister Zoe beside me. We were just born. I'm called a **buck** fawn which means I'm a boy. My sister is called a **doe** fawn. We each weigh around six to seven pounds, the same as a newborn baby. It is late May, and the weather is nice and warm. My mother is licking the both of us and making sure that we are very clean. She does this so that the other animals will not smell my scent and find me.

Before I stand up, I nurse my mother's milk. Wow! That is delicious. Within an hour of my birth, I try to stand up. My legs are so wobbly. I feel a little scared, but I did it. I stood only a few seconds and down I went. I stay with my mother a few hours before Farmer Joe takes me to the deer barn. I then become a **tame** deer instead of a **wild** deer.

Someone is coming toward me. It's Farmer Joe, the man who runs the deer farm. He's taking my twin sister and me to the deer barn. He puts each of us inside a cardboard box with a lot of straw in it. It does feel soft and cozy in here. I guess this will be my new home. Farmer Joe is really gentle with me. He pets both of us and talks to us a lot. This will be a safe place for us. It's nice to have such a warm spot and know my sister is close beside me. I like Farmer Joe!

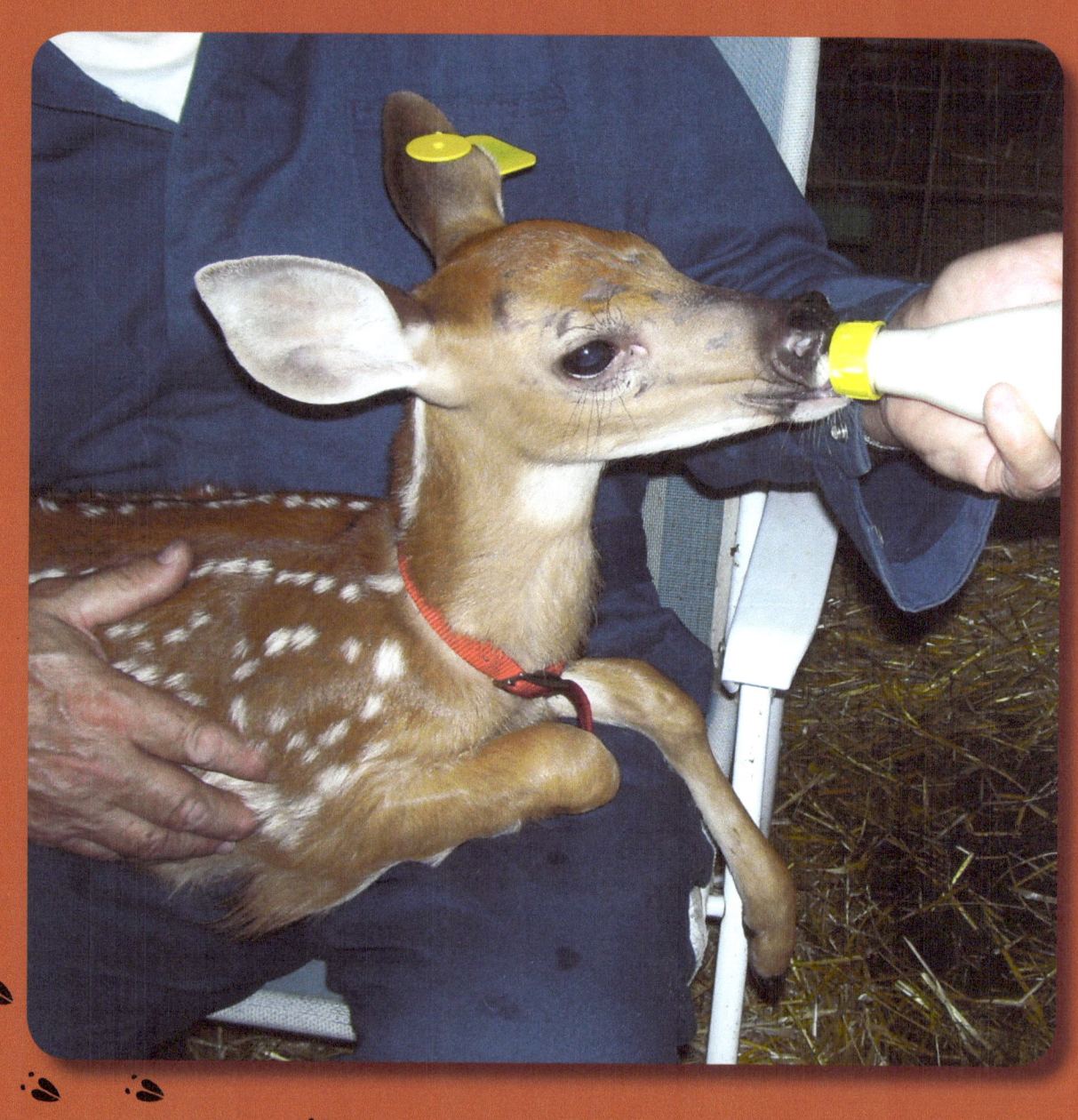

Farmer Joe picks me up and starts to feed me a bottle of warm milk. I don't like it at first. It doesn't smell or feel like my mother's milk. But then Farmer Joe keeps petting and holding me, and I finally take a drink. It is really warm and delicious and tastes really great. I like being held and fed my bottle by Farmer Joe. I feel safe, and I'm drinking a lot more milk each day. Farmer Joe is very special to me.

Growing Up
on a Deer Farm

I'm over a month old now and weigh over twelve pounds. Farmer Joe is still feeding milk to my sister and me. Instead of holding us, he lets us drink from a bucket and share it with a lot of other fawns. It's fun to eat with all of the other deer. I can drink as much as I want and when I want to. I will grow stronger and bigger every day. Once in a while Farmer Joe gives my sister and me a bottle of milk, so he can hold us. That's very, very special.

We also get to go into a fenced pen in the pasture and eat grass every evening. The grass feels great on my two toes which are protected by a hard covering called a *hoof*. The hooves help me push off the ground as I run to get my exercise. I love to run and jump. The other fawns are with us too, and it's great to play with them. What fun!

Every time children come to the deer farm, Farmer Joe lets them feed me from a bottle. I guess he thinks I'm one of the tamest of all the fawns. It's fun to have a little special attention and a lot of extra milk to drink. Sometimes he even puts a collar and leash on me, and they lead me around the yard. Not all of the other fawns are as tame as I am and do not like to be led. But, I do, because it is fun to play in the yard. I feel really special!!

I'm now about two months old and still have my spotted coat. I'm starting to eat alfalfa hay and Farmer Joe's special deer feed. It has corn, oats, molasses and lots of vitamins to make me strong. I get to eat as much as I want. I am still drinking my milk from a bottle at times and also from the bucket with the other deer. I really feel grown up when I'm eating the special deer feed. Yum! Yum! I will become stronger and bigger each day.

I'm really growing, and I'm about four months old now. I only drink milk once a day and eat Farmer Joe's special deer feed and lots and lots of alfalfa hay. My spots are beginning to fade, and pretty soon, they will be all gone. I once had about 300 spots. When my spots are all gone, I won't be reddish-brown anymore. I will be getting my new winter coat and will have more patches of gray and black on my back.

It's early autumn, and I'm not drinking milk from the bottle anymore. My spots are gone, and I feel something growing on top of my head. It is very hard bone, and there is one on each side of my head. Some people think these are horns, but they really are the start of my huge antlers. I am a young buck right now, and my antlers are very small. That's another buck with me in the field. We are called **button bucks** because our small antlers look like little buttons on our head. Every year from now on my antlers will grow bigger and bigger.

I have been growing all winter, and now it is early spring. I feel my new antlers beginning to grow, and my old antlers will soon fall off or **shed**, as my new ones come through. This will happen to me every year from now on, as new antlers re-grow every year. My antlers will look like this my second year and will be even bigger each year from now on. I am now called a four- point buck and considered a yearling buck.

Every year in late autumn, my antlers are almost done growing. They are covered with a thick, soft skin called **velvet**. This skin contains the blood vessels that nourish my antlers until they are fully grown. After they are fully grown, the velvety skin starts to dry up and peel off. I will try to get rid of the hanging velvet by rubbing it off on trees and bushes until nothing is left but hard, shiny bone.

A few years from now, I hope to look just like my dad and have really big antlers. I will then weigh about two hundred pounds. My antlers will have around ten to twelve **points** called **tines**. They branch off the main antlers. This set of antlers is sometimes called a **rack**. I still go up to the fence in the deer pen and eat carrots, apples or bread from Farmer Joe's hand. There are always a lot of fawns born every year, and I can't believe I was one of those fawns just a few years ago. Yes, I'm now considered a BIG BUCK and am as big as my dad. I look just like him!!

DEDICATED TO MY GRANDCHILDREN:

Rachel

Luke

Brock

Jackson

Cade

Photographs by Karen Shellhaas

Graphic Design by Angie Siefring

www.deerfawnbook.com